45 strange & striking ways to get your point across to teenagers

everyday object lessons
for youth groups

Helen Musick Duffy Robbins

Easy-prep ideas for Sunday school, Bible studies, youth talks & more!

Youth Specialties

ZondervanPublishingHouse
Grand Rapids, Michigan
A Division of HarperCollinsPublishers

Everyday Object Lessons for Youth Groups: 45 strange & striking ways to get your point across to teenagers

Copyright © 1999 by Youth Specialties

Youth Specialties Books, 300 S. Pierce St., El Cajon, CA 92020, are published by Zondervan Publishing House, 5300 Patterson Ave. S.E., Grand Rapids, MI 49530.

Library of Congress Cataloging-in-Publication Data

Musick, Helen, 1957-
    Everyday object lessons for youth groups : 45 strange and striking ways to get your point across to teenagers / Helen Musick & Duffy Robbins.
        p. cm.
    Includes index.
    ISBN 0-310-22652-X
    1. Church group work with teenagers. 2. Object-teaching. I. Robbins, Duffy. II. Title.
BV4447.M845 1999
268' .433--dc21   98-55278
                                                                                    CIP

Unless otherwise indicated, all Scripture quotations are taken from the Holy Bible: *New International Version* (North American Edition). Copyright © 1973, 1978, 1984 by International Bible Society. Used by permission of Zondervan Publishing House.

Edited by Vicki Newby and Tim McLaughlin
Cover design by DesignPoint, Inc.
Interior design by Rogers Design & Associates
Illustrations by Rick Sealock

Printed in the United States of America

06 07 08 09 10 • 25 24 23 22 21 20 19 18 17 16

contents

17 No prep & low prep

Everyone has this stuff lying around the house. At worst, you can pick up the objects cheap at the grocery store, drug store, Home Depot, or Toys-R-Us.

91 Some prep, for big results

You may have to make a phone call or two to get your hands on these objects. Then again, they just might be sitting in your closet or garage.

103 Serious prep for special events

If you have these objects around the house, you're either a crackpot or a felon. To borrow them, you'll need to put on your suave salesperson persona. Or have a connection. But the dynamite effect on your kids is worth the considerable preparation. You'll probably want to save these for big or special events.

All about object lessons
& how to use them

Helen: Two years ago my understanding of teaching adolescents changed dramatically when—

Duffy: Me too! Well, it was more than two years ago. The fact that teenagers learn differently than I thought hit me for the first time on a Sunday morning several years ago.

Helen: Okay, so upstage me...

Duffy: I had just finished preaching what I felt was a fairly effective sermon, and people were streaming out of the church. I was in my thanks-for-coming handshake mode, responding to comments as people walked down the front steps of the church.
"I appreciate the encouragement."
"I'm glad you found it helpful."
"No, ma'am, I'm fine, I just haven't been getting much sleep lately."
"Good to see you too."
"Yes, honey, that's my real hair. Shouldn't you be in the nursery?"
Then, came an epiphany.
I got exactly three comments on my sermon—and two of them weren't even about the sermon. They were about the *children's talk* I had given earlier in the service. Now I understand that every sermon isn't going to be a direct hit, but I know good stuff when I hear it, and I thought this was pretty good stuff! A Swindoll outline, two Campolo illustrations, a little John Stott, a bit of Eugene Peterson, and a pinch of Max Lucado. Vintage Duffy Robbins, right?
But I heard no end of conversational references to "Gary the Glove," the object lesson I had used in the children's talk—a simple illustration using a glove and my hand. Middle-aged men in suits were saying, "Hey, that little talk about Gary the Glove really helped."
Gary the Glove? That one-minute object lesson?

Helen: My turn. Over the past 16 years I had worked in the local church pastoring and discipling youths. The students I worked with mostly came from middle and upper-middle class homes. The churches I served were like any traditional church found in the Bible Belt.

All that changed when I accepted a new youth ministry position. Most of my new students came from backgrounds of abuse, neglect, and brokenness.

I remember driving to meet my new youth group for the first time. I had to drive through a security gate and past security guards to a building surrounded by barbed wire fences. My new youth group, 15 girls between the ages of 13 and 17, consisted of young women who, because of crimes they had committed, were now serving time in a full-security rehabilitation facility. With these young women I learned the value of using object lessons as an effective means of teaching adolescence.

I realized quickly that their attention spans were short and their interest levels were low. One week I brought in a sack of shoes: old shoes, new shoes, my daughter's princess dress-up shoes. There were running shoes, infant shoes, fuzzy slippers, and high-heeled pumps. I dumped the shoes out in the middle of the floor.

"Tell me, ladies. If you were to choose one pair of shoes to describe how you feel about life, which pair would it be?" An amazing thing happened. The girls started choosing shoes, and with the most enthusiasm I'd seen yet, they started sharing why they chose the shoes they did.

After the sharing came to an end, I talked to the girls about how Jesus has walked were we've all walked. He's been afflicted, challenged, hurt in the same ways we have. They made the connection, and I saw sparks of insight and interest I had not seen before. The shoes had been a tool to teach these students about God's care and love for them.

Girls who chose not to attend Bible study that night watched from a distance with a level of curiosity that

- Need an object lesson to illustrate the *topic or principle* you're teaching? See the Quick Object Lesson Locator by Topic on page 11.

- Need an object lesson *based on the Bible passage* you're teaching? See the Quick Object Lesson Locator by Scripture Reference on page 12.

- Want to find an object lesson for *the object you have*? See the Quick Object Lesson Locator by Object on page 13.

- Want to find a particular object lesson *whose title you know*? See the Quick Object Lesson Locator by Title on page 15.

eventually led them into the circle.

The next week I brought a bag of jelly beans. And so it went. Many of these object lesson came from a special season of ministry for me—a season I'll always be grateful for.

❖❖❖❖❖

You don't have to work with troubled youths for object lessons to be effective. And object lessons aren't just for children. Since we started working with teenagers, we've incorporated visual objects in sermons for teens and adults alike. The response is always the same: their interest is held and learning occurs. What more could you ask for?

Concrete, visible, vivid, and memorable—it's hard to beat a good object lesson when you're trying to help people understand a biblical truth. To borrow from Paul's words in Colossians 1, object lessons are a kind of visible expression of the invisible, made even more effective by applying the following reminders.

• **The power of an object lesson is in its simplicity.** Resist the temptation to explain all the deep symbolism you've been able to uncover. One of the quickest ways to ruin an object lesson is try to make it more than it is. Make just one truth visible to your students—that's enough. Don't press the analogy so hard that you end up squashing it flat. Mickey Mouse is *not* a Christ figure, Barney is *not* an archetype of socioeconomic oppression, and—even if there are three different fibers in the fabric— Gary the Glove is not about the Trinity. So keep it simple, prepare the best lesson you can, and remember that it's the Holy Spirit, not your object lesson, that instructs and changes students.

> In each object lesson you'll find—
>
> • the *topic*—that is, what topic or principle that object lesson illustrates
> • the *object(s)* you need
> • a *lesson*—what to do with the object, with suggested applications of the lesson to your students' lives
> • a *Bible reference* or two—and usually some extra ones, in case you want to spend even more time in the Bible. (Read the passages ahead of time, then use those verses that highlight the idea you want to emphasize.)
> • *questions* of two kinds: "Discussion Starters," for helping your kids think more deeply and discuss more openly about the topic. And "Life Changers," for helping your kids apply the topic to their own experiences and faith.

• **Gary the Glove is no substitute for Isaiah the Prophet or Paul the Apostle.** Object lessons are a means to an end—an animated illustration used to demonstrate a specific point, make it memorable, or help us apply it. It is not a substitute for biblical truth. The object lessons in this book aren't merely cute props for heart-warming youth talks, but rather tools that will grab the attention and imagination of students long enough for the light of God's truth to penetrate their lives. If we hope to nurture authentic disciples of Christ, we need to develop in our students an appetite for the Word (as the apostle Paul reminds a young church pastor in 2 Timothy 2:15). An object lesson can act as a flashlight, throwing unexpected light on biblical truth.

For each object lesson in this book, we've listed a relevant Bible passage or two —and usually some extras if you want to spend even more time in the Bible. Read the passages ahead of time, then use those verses that highlight the ideas you want to emphasize. Passages from both the Old and New Testaments have been listed to help students understand that both parts of the modern Bible still apply to their attitudes, their behavior, and their faith. And use the Quick Object Lesson Locator by Scripture Reference on page 12 when you're teaching a Scripture passage and need a fitting object lesson.

• **Object lessons don't teach themselves.** No object lesson is so good that the only instruction is "Just add kids." And few ideas work with every group every time. An object lesson is a tool— which means that, for each object lesson, you'll need to think about how it might best be used with *your* kids. Tweak it, shift the emphasis, swap objects . . . you haven't violated any law if you take any of these object lessons in a completely different direction. That's creativity, and it's a *good* thing! (And you can use the ideas in this book to stimulate the creation of your own object lessons.)

• **The point of an object lesson is that kids learn a lesson.** If you stand up with a pair of boxers and say, "You know, life is like a pair of underwear. Let's close in prayer," you're not accomplishing very much. The object isn't the end in itself, but the means to an end. Use objects and object lessons to focus the kids' minds and hearts on spiritual truths.

Each object lesson in this book involves an *object* and some suggested directions to take a *lesson*. We've given you both because you need both. Presenting an object lesson without taking the time to explore the analogy is going to leave them remembering an object instead of a spiritual truth.

In each case we've given you two types of reflection questions. **Discussion Starters** are questions designed to help your kids think about the truth in general terms. What are the implications of this truth? How does it play out in real life? How does this object help us to understand what God is saying in the Bible? To prompt better discussions, we've intentionally avoided simple yes-or-no questions.

A second set of questions we called **Life Changers**—they're designed to take your students to the next stage in the process by asking, "What does this truth mean for me personally?" As the apostle James put it, there's little value in hearing the Word if it doesn't lead to obeying it (James 1:22). The work of helping students apply the truth to their own lives must be done gently (1 Thessalonians 2: 6-8), but it must be done. The doctor who moves her stethoscope from place to place, moves her hand from gland to gland, tugs at the ear, and inspects the throat is not being pushy—she's being thorough. So don't be afraid to probe: "Does it hurt here? How does that feel? Does this relieve the pain?"

• **An object lesson is a tool.** Much like windows, object lessons let us view what we may have missed otherwise. They're for illustration and illumination—a way of letting the light shine through so your kids can look out across the landscape of God's truth.

Unfortunately, it's possible to make an object lesson so elaborate, intense, or distracting that it obscures the truth you want to teach. I remember a young youth ministry intern who, as an object lesson, he hurled a china plate to the floor, sending glass shards flying into the first row of teenagers—and actually cutting one girl. Another girl was so jolted by the sudden crash, she began crying. It was such a powerful illustration that to this day none of those students can remember the point of the demonstration.

Jesus constantly used objects to explaining truths—flowers, birds, water, yeast. One of the most common phrases in the Gospels is "The kingdom of God is like—" But every time he picked up a stalk of wheat or cursed a fig tree or washed filthy feet, he did it to make truth clear. He wasn't trying to intrigue followers with wheat, make disciples sympathetic toward fig trees, or teach people hygiene. He demonstrated spiritual truths with tangible objects so that listeners could understand the truths—and be changed by them.

• **Even the best object lesson won't always work the way you want it to.** Jesus was the master teacher. He spent three years in intense ministry with a handful of disciples. But all too often, when the lesson was over, they were scratching their heads unable to grasp his point. "That was powerful, Jesus! What did it mean?"

Don't be discouraged if your kids respond differently than you want them to. They won't always realize how profound the truth is (a common problem in youth ministry)! Give it another try later on, trust the truth, and trust God to make an impact even when you don't see it happening.

And, of course, make time *somewhere* in your preparation to pray. (Maybe it sounds trite, but you know the power of it.) As far as the spiritual impact on your students is concerned, an ingenious object lesson will fall flat on its face unless it's energized by the power of God.

Demonstrating to the prophet Ezekiel that power, God thought up what may be the mother of all object lessons: looking over a landscape of bleached human bones, God spoke—then, in a clatter and a rattle, those bones became whole skeletons held together with tendons, flesh covered the skeletons, breath entered the bodies—and those bleached bones had become a vast army of animated, breathing individuals.

In the same way may the living God make the dry bones of our best efforts come to life and bear fruit in the lives of our students.

by topic

Quick Object Lesson Locator
by Scripture reference
(page numbers in parentheses)

Genesis 3:1-6 **(38)**

Exodus 7-11 **(22)**

Exodus 20:5-6 **(100)**

Numbers 14 **(70)**

Deuteronomy 32:2 **(58)**

1 Samuel 16:6-7 **(18)**

Psalm 9 **(110)**

Psalm 10 **(110)**

Psalm 11 **(110)**

Psalm 12 **(110)**

Psalm 15 **(110)**

Psalm 19:14 **(34)**

Psalm 20:1-9 **(94)**

Psalm 32:5 **(48)**

Psalm 34:8 **(60)**

Psalm 37:23-24 **(98)**

Psalm 40:1-2 **(96)**

Psalm 56:13 **(96)**

Psalm 66 **(110)**

Psalm 119:4 **(110)**

Psalm 119:133 **(88)**

Proverbs 13:11 **(80)**

Isaiah 40:28-31 **(36)**

Isaiah 52:7 **(96)**

Jeremiah 18:1-6 **(68)**

Amos 2:4-5 **(44)**

Micah 6:8 **(30)**

Matthew 6:19-21 **(108)**

Matthew 6:19-34 **(64)**

Matthew 7:1-5 **(84)**

Matthew 7:15-20 **(44)**

Matthew 12:33-37 **(104)**

Matthew 14:29-32 **(94)**

Matthew 16:26 **(106)**

Mark 4:1-20 **(58)**

Mark 8:34-38 **(56)**

Luke 9:59-62 **(20)**

Luke 12:16-26 **(108)**

Luke 12:33-34 **(64)**

Luke 18:18-25 **(64)**

John 14:6 **(66)**

John 15:5-6 **(72)**

Acts 4:12 **(66)**

Acts 10:1-23 **(86)**

Romans 7:22 **(54)**

Romans 8:18-38 **(52)**

Romans 8:22-28 **(60)**

Romans 12:1-2 **(68)**

Romans 12:1-2 **(70)**

1 Corinthians 5:9-11 **(46)**

1 Corinthians 10:13 **(24)**

1 Corinthians 10:13 **(50)**

2 Corinthians 2:14-15 **(78)**

2 Corinthians 4:7-12 **(52)**

2 Corinthians 6:14-15 **(46)**

2 Corinthians 7:9-10 **(22)**

Galatians 2:20 **(72)**

Galatians 3:26-28 **(62)**

Quick Object Lesson Locator
by object

Quick Object Lesson Locator

by title

No prep & low prep

Everyone has this stuff lying around the house. At worst, you can pick up the objects cheap at the grocery store, drug store, Home Depot, or Toys-R-Us.

Don't Judge a Kiwi by Its Cover

The topic Inner and outer beauty

The object A kiwi and three or four other types of fruit.

The lesson Show students the fruits, one by one, and ask them which they think is the best-looking fruit. (If it's within your and your group's tolerances, it might be fun to have a fruit fashion show—a banana-burlesque of sorts, in which the banana or other fruit gets a little carried away and unpeels a bit.)

Now ask the students

which is the ugliest fruit. Pass around the kiwi so students can touch (and perhaps taste) the outside of the kiwi. It's rough, tough, and tasteless. Then pass around slices  of the kiwi's fruit—and they'll discover it's deliciously sweet.

Like the kiwi, what we see on the outside is seldom an accurate indicator of what's on the inside.

The Word   1 Samuel 16:6-7; James 2:1-9

Discussion starters

1. What makes the kiwi look less appealing?

2. What are some of the outward factors by which we judge others?

3. Who are some of the "kiwi people" in our society? In your school?

4. What are some of the marks of "kiwi beauty" (inner beauty despite a plain or even rough exterior) that God looks for in a person he can use?

Life changers

1. In what ways and with which groups of people are you tempted to concentrate more on your outward appearance?

2. What are some of the kiwi qualities that you need to cultivate so that God can use you better?

3. What steps can you take **this week to get to know the inside of one person you have been avoiding** because of a rough, unappealing exterior?

Rearview Living

The topic Regret

The object A car's rearview mirror. The mirror can probably be removed easily by loosening the set-screw that holds the mirror in its bracket.

The lesson Safe drivers keep a frequent eye on their rearview mirrors. But drivers who *stare* at the rearview mirror won't stay on the road for very long.

Looking at one's **past is valuable. God can use your retrospection— good times and bad, the painful memories as** well as the delicious ones, the hard lessons learned and the hard victories won.

But *staring* into your past is a hazard. When we're too focused on where we've been, we lose track of where we're going. We get off course, and we may end up running into something. Avoid rearview living that keeps your life focused too much on the past, instead of living in the present and looking to the future.

The Word Philippians 3:13b-14; Luke 9:59-62

Discussion starters

1. What are some of the ways looking into the rearview mirror helps a person to drive more safely?

2. Anybody here ever get so focused on the car behind you that you almost crashed into the car in front of you?

3. In what ways can looking back to our past be a good thing? In what ways can it be unhealthy?

4. What are some of the reasons—both good and bad—that we look back on our lives?

5. The apostle Paul talks about "forgetting what is behind." How realistic is that?

6. How do we make sure we bury our past without burying it alive?

Life changers

1. What are some of the memories in your "rearview mirror" that might keep you from moving ahead?

2. How do you deal with the painful stuff you see in your rearview mirror?

3. Some side rearview mirrors read, **"Warning: objects may be closer than they appear."** If you were to place a warning on the rearview mirror of your life, what would it be?

4. What are some steps *you* can take to get your eyes more focused on where you're going and less on where you've been?

Learning from Hard Knocks

The topic Learning the hard way, repentance

The object Get one or two battery-operated or wind-up trucks or cars that move in one direction until they bump into an obstacle and then reverse directions. When you do this object lesson with your group, you may want to seat your students in a circle so the cars operate within the circle. Then, while the cars are bumping into your students and reversing direction, you can present the object lesson.

The lesson These cars are a combination of batteries, aluminum, teeny rubber tires, a few small metal sprockets, and an inch or two of wire. But what makes the toy so intriguing is that it

never gives up—it never stops running, even when it crashes into an obstacle— and when it does, it's smart enough to turn around and choose another course.

Sometimes, when we're in pursuit of a worthy goal, we find we have to keep moving ahead, even when we run into obstacles. Then perseverance is a *good* thing. But more often we run into obstacles and crash into stuff because we've gotten off course. In cases like that, to keep banging our heads against the wall is a *bad* thing. Sometimes God uses the negative circumstances and hard knocks in our lives to get our attention so we can see our need to turn around.

The Word Exodus 7-11 (Note especially how Pharaoh, hard-hearted and hard-headed, was willing to endure all kinds of plagues before he would release the people of Israel from their bondage in Egypt as God had commanded.); 2 Corinthians 7:9-10 *See also Acts 9:1-18; Luke 15:11-24; Proverbs 14:12*

Discussion starters
1. Why do we keep doing things that get us nowhere and continue to hurt us?
2. Why do you suppose Pharaoh, who had already agreed to let the people of Israel go, decided to wait one more day to do so even though it meant spending one more night with the frogs (see Exodus 8:2-10)? Why is it some people never learn except in the school of hard knocks?
3. When you're facing an obstacle, how do you know whether you should try harder or turn around?

4. What are some of the walls we run into **when we get off the course of God's will?**
5. How is changing course, or turning around, like what the Bible says about repentance?
6. What is the difference between *regret* and *repent* (see 2 Corinthians 7:9-10)?

Life changers
1. Are there any obstacles in your life that God might be using to change your course (lousy relationships with parents, problems with friends, trouble with the law, betrayal, bad health, bad grades, guilt)?
2. What are some of the reasons that you might be choosing to spend another night with the frogs?
3. Enduring the plagues, living in a pig sty, kicking against the goads—all these once seemed right. Do you need to rethink the course you're on today and turn around? What would it take to get you to change your course?

Sun Block & Son Block

The topic God's Son protects us

The object Sunblock in different colors and brands and, if possible, pictures of skin cancer (possibly from your local doctor's office or the local office of the American Cancer Society). This is a great object lesson for a day at the beach or by the pool.

The lesson We're given countless warnings on TV and in magazines about the dangers of prolonged exposure to the sun **and how it may result in skin cancer. And yet we continue to bask in the sun, lie on the beach, and soak up the rays. In fact, when we see someone who's tan, we often think to ourselves,** "Wow, I'd love to have a tan like that." In our culture a

good tan is a symbol of good health, good looks, the lifestyle of the rich and famous. We have a hard time accepting the fact that a good tan can lead to bad health; dried up, wrinkled skin; and death. Skin cancer often starts as a small spot that looks like a mole, but it grows deep and deadly.

What we seldom read about in magazines or hear about on TV or even from the medical community is an even graver danger: *sin* cancer. It also may start as a small spot, usually in the heart, but grows just like skin cancer until the whole body is affected. Most people don't even notice the sin cancer growing at first. In fact, sometimes the people it's growing in are the ones who seem the coolest, the most suave, and the hippest people we know. Who would guess that later on, like aging skin that has been exposed for too many years to the sun, the end result might be ugly wrinkles in the memory, a parched heart, lesions of guilt, and eventually death?

The good news is that God has provided sin-block protection for us, and it's based on prolonged exposure to his Son. His protection is a beauty secret that goes way below the pigment of the skin and deals with the darkness of the human heart. It's a pattern of life that says, "Lord, I need you to help me screen out the temptation and sin in my life." It's a lifestyle of health that begins with stepping out of the darkness of sin by walking, living, and basking in the light of God's Son.

The Word Ephesians 5:8-14; 1 John 1:7-9
See also 1 Corinthians 10:13; 2 Corinthians 4:4-17; Matthew 4:16; 6:13

Discussion starters
1. Why is it that we are warned so often about skin cancer but almost never hear any public health warnings about sin cancer? Which has caused more damage and death on this planet?
2. Skin cancer first appears on the skin as small moles or patches of skin. What are some of the symptoms of sin cancer?

3. How can God protect us from **exposure to sin?**

Life changers
1. There are certain times of day when prolonged and unprotected exposure to the sun is especially dangerous. When are you at greatest risk—during your day or week—of the kind of exposures that might lead to sin cancer?
2. Most people begin applying sun block by rubbing it onto the nose and face, and then moving to the shoulders, back, and legs. Are there some parts of your life that need to be better protected from sin with Son block? What are they (dating, cheating, anger, entertainment, lying, relationship with parents)?

Fuming in the Heart & Foaming at the Mouth

The topic Anger.

The object Four students; Alka-Seltzer (*note that Alka-Seltzer contains asprin and may cause an allergic reaction for those who are allergic to asprin*), a two-liter bottle of 7-Up, four clear cups, and four plastic trash bags.

The lesson Get four students up to the front with you. Have each of them hold a spoonful of Alka-Seltzer in one hand, and a cup of the 7-Up in the other. Set a garbage bag in front of each of them, too, so that what's about to happen won't happen all over the youth room. Explain to the four that, when you say when, they'll spoon the Alka-Seltzer into their mouths, then drink in—*but not swallow*, otherwise they'll explode—*all* of the soda (that's why the cup is clear). The contest? To see who can hold the frothy mixture in his mouth the longest before erupting and spewing.

We're instructed by the Scripture to deal with our anger

quickly, because if we try to hold it in, fuming and foaming, it will eventually come spewing out as

"bitterness, rage and anger, brawling and slander, along with every form of malice."

The Word   Ephesians 4:26-27, 31-32

Discussion starters

1. "In your anger do not sin," writes the apostle Paul to the Ephesian Christians. That's a command, not a suggestion. But how do you keep anger from becoming sinful?

2. What are some ways that your refusal to deal with anger—by trying to stuff it inside, by denying that you're angry when it's obvious to everyone else that you are—gives the devil an opportunity?

3. Why do we let the sun go down on our anger?

4. How do we resolve disagreements with our friends without leaving a big mess and a bad taste in everyone's mouth?

Life changers

1. You've heard the line, "Don't get mad—get even." But some people don't get mad *or* even—instead they get new friends or get quiet or get out of the youth group. How do *you* deal with anger? Does your method of dealing with anger give the devil an opportunity to create problems?

2. Is there someone right now you're having a tough time with? Write a letter to that person right now, trying to clear away the anger before the sun goes down again on another day.

Clogged Filters & Cluttered Minds

The topic Discernment

The object Different kinds of clean and dirty filters—automobile air or oil filters (auto tune-up shops always have old dirty ones lying around), furnace or air conditioning filters, clothes dryer filters, swimming pool filters.

The lesson A good filter allows air, water, oil—whatever's being filtered—to flow through it, but keeps the dirty particles from passing through. That's what *discernment* is—a mind filter. The ability to

screen out what's false and accept what's true. From what St. Paul tells us in Ephesians 4:14, discernment is a big part of spiritual maturity.

The Word Philippians 1:9-11; Philippians 4:8-9
See also Ephesians 4:14

Discussion starters
1. What's the difference between a mind that's open enough to consider new ideas, and a mind with a gaping hole that let's absolutely *everything* in?
2. How can your mind filter get messed up?
3. How can you clean out and clean up a clogged, malfunctioning mind filter (for example, Romans 12:1-2)?

Life changers

1. Any of the following explain why your mind filter might be getting clogged up?

- ○ HBO
- ○ MTV
- ○ NPR
- ○ *Elle*
- ○ *Rolling Stone*
- ○ *Seventeen*
- ○ GQ
- ○ *Mad*
- ○ General Hospital
- ○ Ally McBeal
- ○ Allan McNeal (your neighbor)
- ○ Leonardo Di Caprio
- ○ Leonardo da Vinci
- ○ Danielle Steele
- ○ Stephen King

(If you want less humorous, more open-ended choices for your students to respond to, try these instead:)

- ○ Movies I watch
- ○ Music I listen to
- ○ Books and magazines I read
- ○ Friends I spend time with
- ○ Other?

2. Considering what it is that's clogging up your mind filter, how do you go about cleaning it? In other words, **how do you renew your mind, as St. Paul recommends in Romans 12:1-2?**

3. If you took Philippians 4:8-9 seriously in your own life, how might your daily life be different? What might you have to change?

If the Shoe Fits

The topic Walking with Christ daily

The object Shoes of all styles, sizes, and colors—the more bizarre, the better. You can find a wide selection for next to nothing at a thrift shop. Try to get at least these kinds: work boots, bedroom slippers, dress shoes, running shoes, a pair that is totally worn out, a pair with holes in the soles.

The lesson Show the shoes one pair at a time, explaining **how they can help us consider where we are in our walk with Christ:**

Dress shoes	I have a nice, shiny faith on the outside—but I only bring it out on Sundays and special occasions.
Bedroom slippers	I've made a commitment to Christ, but I've been pretty lazy in terms of trying to serve him.

Work boots	It's been hard work lately, but I'm actually following through on my responsibilities.
Running shoes	I feel like God's helping me finish the race.
Worn out shoes	I've come a long way, but I need some serious "heeling."
Holey shoes	I don't worry too much about a relationship with God or the state of my soul.

The Word   Micah 6:8; Colossians 2:6-7
See also Ephesians 6:14-15

Discussion starters
1. Which of the shoes do you think most represents our youth group?

2. What type of shoes would **you wear to "walk humbly with your God"?**

Life changers
1. Which of the shoes best represents your own walk with Christ right now?

Monuments or footprints?

The topic Christian life as a journey

The object Make footprints this way: mix a small batch of poster paint, and pour it into a shallow container. Dip an old boot or shoe in the paint and make a footprint on a piece of paper. Find a miniature monument or landmark of some kind. For example, you can buy a miniature Washington Monument, Statue of Liberty, Gateway Arch (St. Louis), Sears Tower (Chicago), the Alamo, Space Needle (Seattle), Golden Gate Bridge, Cape Canaveral, Chimney Rock (western Nebraska).

The lesson You can think about the Christian life in two ways: 1) always pointing back to some monumental experience—last summer at camp or last February on the **ski weekend or when I was a child in vacation Bible school. That approach to the Christian life is best symbolized by a monument.**

Or 2) looking at it as a journey, an adventure that continues to unfold. Instead of looking back to experiences that happened last year or last summer or 30 years ago when I first joined this church, it's an attitude that enjoys what God is doing in my life right now and looks ahead toward where he's leading me—an attitude best symbolized by a footprint.

Not that there's anything wrong with looking back toward monumental experiences. Just make sure it's a milestone or marker, not a tombstone. There are already too many Christians who are justified, sanctified, and petrified.

The Word   Philippians 3:12-14

Discussion starters

1. How do we "forget what is behind" **without totally forgetting what God has done for us and taught us in the past?**

2. What does Paul mean by "straining toward what is ahead"?

Life changers
1. Which best summarizes your life: the monument or the footprint?

Bonus!
Give students a paper with the text of Philippians 3:12-14 printed across the bottom, then let them make their own footprints on it—using their own shoes or their own bare feet. Or make a "baby footprint" (it's a little easier than an actual footprint, too): make a fist, and set it in the paint as you would slam your fist on a table (but don't slam your fist in the paint!). You'll have an uncanny, convincing infant's footprint. Create small prints this way on heavy stock, cut out around them, and kids will have a convenient, pocket-sized footprint they can use as Bible bookmarks or otherwise carry around with them as reminders to keep on walkin' toward the goal.

Or use the same methods to make a huge mural for the youth room, with all the kids' footprints on the mural. Paint the text of Philippians 3:12-14 across the bottom of the banner.

Say Ahhhhhh

The topic Words can hurt or help

The object Popsicle sticks. For extra fun, videotape (or shoot with a Polaroid) the tongue-examination part of the lesson.

The lesson Pass out the popsicle sticks and pair up students. Tell them to examine their partner's tongue. Next, give them five **minutes to write a poem about the tongue they inspected. Award the best writer with a popsicle.**

Scripture tells us the tongue does for us what a rudder does for a ship: although it's small and out of view most of the time, it nevertheless steers our lives and others' lives.

The Word James 3:3-5; Psalm 19:14

Discussion starters
1. When is your tongue like a rudder that steers you off course?

2. How can you use your tongue to steer you in a *good* direction?

3. Why is speech such an important part of the disciple's lifestyle?

Life changers

1. How has your conversation led you off course sometime during the past two weeks?

2. Think of three good ways you can speak this week—affirm a teacher, encourage a friend, thank a parent, share your faith with your friends, etc.

Bonus

Close by inviting students to pray one or more of these Bible verses:

● Whoever of you loves life and desires to see many good days, keep your tongue from evil and your lips from speaking lies. —*Psalm 34:12-13 and 1 Peter 3:10*

● The words of the wicked lie in wait for blood, but the speech of the upright rescues them. —*Proverbs 12:6*

● He who loves a pure heart and whose speech is gracious will have the king for his friend. —*Proverbs 22:11*

● Woe to me!...I am ruined! For I am a man of unclean lips, and I live among a people of unclean lips, and my eyes have seen the King, the Lord Almighty. —*Isaiah 6:5*

● Don't let anyone look down on you because you are young, but set an example for the believers in speech, in life, in love, in faith and in purity. —*1 Timothy 4:12*

5K Females & Marathon Men

The topic Christian life as a distance race

The object For this lesson, *you're* the object. Get introduced as distance runner Steve Prefontaine (the fact that he's been dead for nearly 25 years doesn't hurt the usefulness of this object lesson) or Lynn Jennings (or Elva Dryer or Naomi Mugo...check out these runners' bios on the Web if you want to sound like you know who you are). Walk into the room wearing a brightly colored, skin-tight Lycra running suit. What makes this object lesson work is that, either this is *very* different from how the kids usually see you, and/or you look *very* silly dressed this way.

The lesson You probably aren't a distance runner in the sense that you regularly run 5000 meters or a 12K a month. Yet the Bible speaks of a marathon with a prize far more precious than a gold medal.

That marathon is

your **Christian life—a race that begins when you make that first commitment to Christ,** and which continues until the end of your life...and beyond. It's a race you win, not by going fast but by

going far—not by sprinting ahead early in the race, but by keeping up the pace, especially late in the race. It's not about those who've arrived, but about those who've survived.

The Word   Hebrews 12:1-3; Isaiah 40:28-31
See also Philippians 3:12-14

Discussion starters

1. Why do people who started with Christ drop out of the race early?

2. How can you refresh yourself **and replenish your energy in the middle of this marathon of life and faith?**

Life changers

1. Name some of the weights that slow your pace in the race.
2. Which of the following statements sums up your status in this race of faith?
- ○ I'm pressing on toward the goal.
- ○ I tend to get distracted with stuff off the track, instead of keeping my eyes on Christ at the finish line.
- ○ Actually, I haven't entered the race yet.
- ○ I feel like I've got my second wind.
- ○ I feel like I'm gone with the wind.

Joy & Glory under the Kitchen Sink

The topic Fooled by appearances

The object Joy dishwashing detergent, Glory floor cleaner—
and maybe two or three other products with names that promise
more than the product delivers, like Ecstasy cologne, Kool
cigarettes, and Promise margarine.

The lesson Sooner or later, everyone is taken in by packaging
that promises more than the product can deliver. Joy....when did it
become such a hoot to wash dishes? Glory....mop with this stuff
**and you'll
see the
face of
Jesus
appear on
your
bathroom
wall.
Ecstasy...it's
only a
perfume, for
crying out loud.**
When it comes to the hard decisions of real life, Satan
often hits us with this same bait-and-switch, promising us one
thing and giving us something else.

The Word   Genesis 3:1-6 (fruit that was "pleasing to the eye");
Ephesians 4:14 ("cunning and craftiness of men in their deceitful
scheming")
*See also Genesis 13:10 (Lot saw what looked "like the garden of the
Lord," but this was "before the Lord destroyed Sodom and Gomorrah.")*

Discussion starters

1. You see not only products packaged precisely to blur your
thinking, but ideas, too. For example, people talk about "making
love" as if two people having sex will somehow *create* love. What
other ideas are camouflaged by dishonest packaging or
advertising?

2. What false promises does our culture make about alcohol? About sex? Money? Good times? Popularity?

3. How can you see beyond the Joy, Ecstasy, Promise, and Glory
so you don't buy into something you don't need (for example,
Proverbs 3:5-6)?

Life changers

1. Ever been sold a product that doesn't live up to the promise?
What was the sales pitch that hooked you? That it'll be fun? That
it won't hurt you? That everybody else is doing it? That it'll make
you popular? Sexy? Macho? Happy?

Maturity & Manurity

The topic Priorities

The object Manure (cow, horse, goat, rabbit, whatever—in a bag or fresh from the stable), trinkets representing perilous priorities (toy BMW or Expedition, Jaguar, pennies, head of a Barbie doll, CD, scrunchie, golf ball).

The lesson Before the meeting begins, cover a table with newspaper—then bury several trinkets, each under its own little manure pile. Start the object lesson by digging into the piles one at a time to find the object—or have your kids do it. Whether you

dig through the stuff with bare hands or use tongs or gloves is up to you. (Although it goes without saying what will get the best reaction from your students!) When you finally uncover an object, explain what it symbolizes—luxury vehicles, wealth, glamour, music, fashion, sports, etc.

The apostle Paul warns us about the danger of placing excessive value on these things. The sorts of things that the world considers valuable are just trinkets and toys—in fact, just manure—compared to the worth of knowing Christ (Philippians 3:8).

The Word   Philippians 3:7-9 (The Greek word in verse 8 delicately translated as *rubbish* is actually the word for *manure*.)

Discussion starters

1. What could a high schooler **expect to give up in order to gain Christ and be committed to him? In other words, what are the costs of being a Christian in your school?**
2. Is it possible to be a mature, committed Christian and *not* have to give up things like wealth, sports, and glamour?

Life changers
1. What sorts of things would be hardest for you to give up?
2. Imagine a manure-meter that lets you score your progress as you learn to live Philippians 3:8—as you learn to value the things of the world as you'd value poop. What would be your score on a scale of one to ten (10 being "I count *everything* a loss," and 1 being "Well, there's something about manure I still like")? Why would you score yourself that way?

Reflecting on the Reflection

The topic Seeing ourselves as we really are

The object A mirror.

The lesson When you look at yourself in the mirror and notice food in your teeth **or your zipper open or your sweater on backwards or rust on your nose ring—you take immediate action to fix things. The reason you don't ignore such oversights or gaffes is that, thanks to the mirror, you see yourself as others see you.**

Among other things, Scripture is a mirror for you. It helps you see yourself as God sees you—and he wants you to respond to what you see.

The Word   James 1:22-25

Discussion starters

1. Ever walk around school for three or four periods before someone told you that you had toilet paper wrapped around your shoe, or a note stuck on your back that says, "Barney is my main man"?

2. Is it possible to completely **miss seeing a problem in yourself, even if the mirror is right there in front of you?**

3. What are some reasons people avoid looking in the mirror?

Life changers

1. What are some reasons you may avoid looking into the mirror of Scripture?

2. If people were secretly watching you this week, which would they decide is most important to you—how others view you, or how God views you?

3. Do you spend most of your time looking into the wall mirror or the Word mirror?

Careful Who You Run With

The topic Deceptive appearances, wrong choices

The object A Hershey chocolate bar and Ex-Lax. Break off a piece of each so they look similar.

The lesson Hold up both pieces (supposedly, both are chocolate). As you speak, gesture as if you're offering them to this or that student—but never actually let them out of your hand. On the basis of appearances alone, we might be happy to have some of this chocolate for a treat. The result for choosing this one **(show the chocolate) is pleasure, a zit or two, and maybe some extra weight. The result of choosing <u>this</u> one, however (show the Ex Lax), is extra time in the bathroom.**

Appearances can't always tell you what the best choice is.

Scripture warns us that the promises and claims of today's false prophets may seem sweet and tasty—but when we consume their ideas and philosophies, there's turmoil waiting on the inside.

That's why Scripture instructs us to look deeper than just the outside appearance when making choices—to look instead toward the fruit, or result, of the decision. In fact, this one question can save you a lot of grief: *If I make this choice, how will it turn out in the end?* Just like choosing between these very similar looking squares, what you swallow can lead to very different outcomes.

The Word   Matthew 7:15-20; Amos 2:4-5
See also Proverbs 13:5, 21:28

Discussion starters
1. Where in our culture today do you hear the voices of false prophets?

2. What sort of disguises do these false prophets wear (sexy, successful, intellectual)?

3. What kind of lies are false prophets telling us these days?

4. Give examples of "good fruit" and "bad fruit" in your life. What kind of results, or fruit, are you looking for?

Life changers
1. Through which influences are you personally *most* exposed to the lies of the false prophets: Friends? Music? Movies? TV? Family? Magazines? Teachers? Or—?

2. When you're making a decision, are you more inclined to ask, "How do I want this to come out in the end?" or to tell yourself, "This is what I want to consume now"?

3. Think of your own life...have you swallowed any lies of false prophets? Which lies?

Brought Down by a Friend

The topic Choosing friends wisely

The object A table. For safety's sake, make it a low table or chair. (The low-slung furniture in the threes and fours Sunday school classroom is perfect.) Entice a muscular student to stand on the table, and a more delicate student to stand on the floor next to the table. Ask your kids **how easy they think it would be for the less muscular student to push or pull the more muscular student off the chair. (Fairly easy, thanks to** gravity and, if it's a chair the big guy is standing on, the narrow stance that the small seat provides). Probably a *lot* easier to push the big guy off than for the big guy to *lift* the other student up—which is what you ask the big guy to do now. (The lifting part of this object lesson can probably be demonstrated safely, as long as the miniature table or chair is sturdy. Make sure that the big guy you've chosen has to really work at lifting the smaller student off the ground.)

The lesson The point you're after is 1) how *difficult* it is to lift up someone to your higher level, even if you're stronger, and 2) how *easy* it is to be pulled down, despite your strength. The application to the kinds of friends kids choose for themselves is obvious.

The Word 2 Corinthians 6:14-15; 1 Corinthians 5:9-11
See also 1 Corinthians 15:33; Proverbs 22:24-25

Discussion starters
1. Is it easier for a non-Christian to pull a Christian down than it is for a Christian to pull a non-Christian up?
2. If you're not supposed to have "fellowship with darkness," how can you ever help introduce your non-Christian friends to Christ? How do you draw the line between being "salt of the earth"—that is, an agent of Christ at your school—and "not losing your saltiness" so that you're just like everybody else (see Matthew 5:13)? (As you're discussing this with your students, you might have them think about whether the student-on-table situation would change if there were several people on the floor pulling the big guy down, or several people on the table pulling the one person up.)
3. How do you take these biblical warnings seriously and yet be friends with non-Christians?
4. What do these Bible passages mean for people who are in a dating relationship with non-Christians? Is it wrong to date non-Christians? Are there circumstances under which you could rightly date non-Christians?

Life changers
1. In your friendships, which person do you tend to be—the one on the floor, or the one on the table?
2. Do you have any relationships that are pulling you down? What could you do to change the situation?
3. Identify some people in your life whose influence is pulling you up.

Cleansing, Closing, & Confessing

The topic Confession and healing

The object A bottle of hydrogen peroxide, a tourniquet, and bandages of various sizes, shapes, and kinds—including a butterfly bandage

The lesson Each of these bandages helps the healing process **by covering wounds to prevent infection. But before you cover a wound, you need to expose it to someone who can clean it out and, if necessary, close it up.** The best bandage in the world won't help if you don't first kill the bacteria in the wound. Hydrogen peroxide can sterilize the area, and tourniquets can stop severe bleeding.

And in the case of a gash, a butterfly bandage pulls together both sides of the cut so the wound can heal.

The process of cleaning out your emotional wounds and sewing up your hurts and hearts is what the Bible calls *confession.*

Confession is bringing your wounds to Jesus—whether they're rug burns or deep gashes—and asking him to heal them. Instead of asking for hydrogen peroxide on these kinds of wounds, you ask for forgiveness. When two people have a gash in their relationship, they need to come together for emotional healing—which occasionally requires telling a third party—Jesus—about hurts and bruises you've received.

You can't count on Jesus to undo emotional and spiritual wounds—but you can *always* count on him stopping the bleeding. And making it feel better.

The Word 1 John 1:9; Psalm 32:5
See also Proverbs 28:13

Discussion starters
1. Why do we tend to fear exposing our infection and pain to the doctor? What are we afraid of?
2. Why might we prefer to cover up the wound without first cleaning it out?
3. What happens when you cover a wound without first dealing with it properly?

Life changers
1. What wounds do you need to expose to Jesus for healing?
2. What confessions do you need to make to God?

Traps

The topic The lure of temptation

The object A mousetrap (or, for increased effect, a rattrap), cheese (or peanut butter), a toy mouse or rat (plastic or fabric; get one at a pet shop or toy store). Attach the mouse to a stick so your fingers aren't too near the trap. (Of course, if you want to live dangerously—and *really* get the interest of your kids—hold the mouse in your fingers, *really* close to where the trap will snap shut.)

The lesson Manipulate the mouse closer and closer to the cheese-baited trap as you narrate how temptation works with a few typical adolescent temptations—to party, to sleep with a boyfriend, to cheat at school, to lie on little matters. For example, as you describe the way you or your students flirt with sin, have the mouse approach the cheese, take a tentative nibble,

get bolder, take a more aggressive bite, move in a little too close— then SNAP, the trap breaks its neck. The

louder and more unexpected the snap, the more vivid the example will be of the lure and danger of temptation.

Scripture warns us that although temptation itself is not sinful, it *can lead* to getting dragged away and enticed into more temptation—until finally the sin trap is sprung, the bar slams down, and the result is death.

The Word James 1:13-19; 1 Corinthians 10:13
See also 2 Timothy 2:22

Discussion starters
1. What makes a mouse approach a trap?
2. How do James' comments in verses 14 and 15 compare to what you've just witnessed with the killer mousetrap? How is the mouse's situation different from yours? In other words, what keeps you from walking into the trap of temptation?
3. What are some of the cheesy ways you're lured into temptation?
4. What are some of the ways Scripture tells you to spring the sin trap?
5. Present the following passages for your students to consider:
  - 2 Timothy 2:22 *(Get the heck out of Dodge City)*
  - 1 Corinthians 10:13 *(Draw upon Christ's strength to fight temptation)*
  - 1 Corinthians 15:33 *(Don't hang out with people who hang around traps)*
  - John 8:31-32 *(Know the truth about the traps)*
  - 1 Corinthians 6:9-11 *(God can free us from the trap of sin)*

Life changers
1. What kinds of lures entice you into a trap?
2. Do you have any **warning systems to let you know when you're getting lured into the trap of sin? Parents? Friends? Youth pastor? Mr. Rogers?**
3. Which of the following statements best describes your response to the lures of the sin trap?
  - ○ See no evil, smell no evil, hear no evil.
  - ○ So what's wrong with giving the cheese a little sniff?
  - ○ I feel like I'm already trapped.
  - ○ I have a hard time telling the difference between free cheese and a trap.

The Surprises of Brokenness

The topic Good gifts from hard times

The object A piñata. Get one at a craft store, drop by your local Mexican restaurant and ask who makes theirs—or simply inflate a balloon, cover it with papier mâché, let it dry, then make a small hole in its top and fill it with candy.

The lesson At your meeting, hang the piñata by a rope from the ceiling or a tree branch. Invite two students to be blindfolded, then take turns trying to hit the piñata with a stick. The object, of course, is to break it open so the candy falls out for everyone to grab.

During some seasons in life, you feel **like you're just getting beat up, flogged by lousy circumstances. You might as well be a sitting duck—** or a swinging piñata—and life just keeps punching you.

Yet God can use such hits and hurts to bring about a delight and sweetness that might otherwise have remained hidden and untasted. Sometimes the bitterness of disappointment and even pain can become an avenue to the sweet gifts of God.

The Word   Romans 8:18-38; 2 Corinthians 4:7-12
See also Genesis 37-45

Discussion starters
1. What did the apostle Paul experience (see 2 Corinthians 11:25-27)?

2. In what ways **does life stick it to you** during these years?

3. In these passages God doesn't promise you a sweet, easy life. But what *does* God promise?

Life changers
1. What hits have you been taking lately in your own life?

2. Recall a time when your bitter experience turned out to be a sweet gift from God.

3. Think of a friend or family member who's been getting hit lately. Write them a short note of encouragement.

I Feel Good All Under!

The topic Integrity

The object All types and sizes of underwear.

The lesson Remind (or inform) your students about the Hanes underwear commercial, in which a guy is so overwhelmed with the comfort of his Hanes boxers, he announces to everybody in the elevator, "I feel good all under!" At which point all the elevator passengers burst into the Hanes underwear jingle: "Hanes makes you feel good all under" (which happens *so often*, as you've **probably experienced yourself, when you**

brag about your underwear in an elevator). Although people hope we *don't* report the status of our underwear, all of us can still identify with what this guy was so excited about. There's a deep-down comfort when your underwear fits—and a deep-down discomfort when it doesn't.

You have deep-down comfort when you have integrity, and deep-down discomfort when you don't. That's why it's important that your life on the outside (the life that everyone sees) begins with an inward life (the life that others *don't* see). In other words, integrity isn't just *knowing* the truth, it's being *true to what you know*. It's the freedom and confidence that happens when you know people see an "outside you" that matches your "inside you." It's a good feeling, and it starts all under.

The Word   1 John 3:19-22; Romans 7:22
See also Ephesians 3:16; Proverbs 19:21

Discussion starters
1. How would you respond if someone said it shouldn't matter what you think and feel on the *inside*, as long as you do the right thing on the *outside*?
2. Is God more concerned with what we *do*, or about who we *are*? How do you know?

3. What makes it so tough to **maintain your integrity today?**

Life changers
1. To what degree does your "outside you" reflect your inner life and convictions?
2. What kinds of situations really test your integrity as a Christian?

Chasing Bubbles

The topic Pursuing what the world values

The object Two or three types of bubble-making wands and bubble soap.

The lesson As you blow bubbles over the group, talk about how fascinating bubbles are to watch—and how fun they are to make. They come in lots of sizes (depending on your wand, of course), and anyone who can dip and wave can make them. But

all bubbles have this in common: they inevitably pop. Whether you try to hold a bubble, or just let it fly free—sooner or later (usually sooner) it will burst.

The world waves a wandful of fascinating, alluring pictures of fun, romance, happiness, wealth. And for a while, the picture may actually seem real. But sooner or later, just when you think you've finally gotten enough, had enough, or become enough to make life work...just when you thought you might be lifted above the frustrations and difficulties of life, the bubble bursts. You reach out to grab it, and it pops on you.

First things first, the Bible says: seek God and his kingdom. That's first. Everything else will pass away, but the kingdom of God will stick around longer than the Beatles. Lots longer.

The Word   1 John 2:15-17; Mark 8:34-38 (especially v. 35)
See also Matthew 6:31-33; James 4:13-14 (especially in the version The Message)

Discussion starters
1. What kinds of bubbles do students at your school pursue?
2. What makes these bubbles look so appealing?
3. What did the apostle John **mean when he wrote, "Do not love the world or anything in the world"?**
4. What does it look like to "seek first his kingdom"?

Life changers
1. What bubbles are *you* chasing?
2. Complete this statement: *I am seeking* _____ *first.*

Spiritual Lawn Care

The topic Staying fresh spiritually

The object Using a garden trowel or a shovel, dig up two squares of turf—one lush (from the corner of your yard, from the corner of your neighbor's lawn, from an especially lush pasture) and one withered, dry, and scraggly (from the roadside or from your own neglected lawn).

The lesson Scripture tells us that we're like grass. Our lives can **be fresh and green, or they can be dry and withered. The difference is the kind** of care given to maintaining the lawn.

The Word Mark 4:1-20; Deuteronomy 32:2
See also 2 Kings 19:26; Isaiah 37:27

Discussion starters
1. Name some ways we can care for our spiritual lawn.

2. What are some reasons why the seed of the Word doesn't grow and prosper
in our lives (see Mark 4:1-20)?

Life changers
1. What might be making it hard for spiritual seeds to grow in your life?
2. Which method of spiritual lawn care are you willing to use in your own life?
3. How would you describe the condition of your spiritual lawn?
   - ○ My lawn? Hey, it's green and growing.
   - ○ Well, uh, no, I haven't exactly been watering my lawn lately.
   - ○ My lawn is brown.
   - ○ Lawn? I can't even see it for the weeds.
   - ○ I planted one for the first time, but the seeds don't have a chance to grow, they're getting so trampled on by people.

Bonus!
To extend your students' memory of this lesson, give each of them a packet of lawn or flower seeds—along with your own instructions for basic spiritual nurture.

All Things Work Together

The topic The goodness of God's plan

The object Bake one batch of chocolate chip cookies (more batches for larger groups). Collect the ingredients for an additional batch, but keep these ingredients in separate containers.

The lesson Keeping the batch of baked cookies hidden, let different students taste different ingredients—the flour, baking soda, shortening, etc.—without letting them know that it's chocolate chip cookie ingredients they're tasting. Ask them to describe what they taste. (Most of the ingredients taste bitter, slimy, or are tasteless—except for the sugar and chocolate chips, which are usually dead giveaways. So you may not want to let kids taste *these* ingredients.) Surprise them by revealing the already baked cookies, pointing out how something so delicious is made from a mixture of ingredients that are themselves either yucky or bland.

For most of us, life is **a mixture of sweet and bitter seasons, wonderful interludes when everything goes the way we hope, and difficult periods**

when disappointment and discouragement leave a bad taste in our mouths. The wonder of God's sovereignty is that he can combine these circumstances to bring about something good.

The Word   Romans 8:22-28; Psalm 34:8

Discussion starters
1. What would the cookies taste like if we left out the bitter ingredients and included only the sweet ones?

2. What does the Scripture mean by "for the good of those who love him"
(Romans 8:28)?

Life changers
1. What are some bitter experiences that have been mixed into your life?
2. What are some sweet ingredients you can thank God for?
3. Write a letter to God thanking him for the goodness of his plan.

Chocolate Chip Cookies

1 cup brown sugar
1 cup white sugar
1 cup shortening
1 large egg
3 teaspoons vanilla
2 cups plus 4 tablespoons flour
1 teaspoon baking soda
2 cups chocolate chips

Mix the brown sugar, white sugar, and shortening. Add the egg and vanilla. Combine the flour and baking soda together and then add into the sugar mixture. Stir in the chocolate chips. Drop by spoonfuls onto a cookie sheet. Bake at 350 degrees for 8 to 10 minutes.

Jelly Bean Bigots

The topic Racism

The object Jelly beans in assorted flavors.

The lesson Put out *lots* of jelly beans, of *lots* of flavors—then let your kids at 'em. After a couple minutes take an informal voice poll of favorite flavors. You'll probably hear comments like "I hate the banana jelly beans—they stink"…"No way, I love the banana ones. They rock!" If flavor loyalties run deep in your group, you might want to make the poll "official" by tabulating the results on a white board.

It won't take long for everyone to see just how subjective taste is. What one person thinks is delicious is another's loathing. Just because one person or a nation of persons likes (or dislikes) or appreciates (or depreciates) something, doesn't make that something good or bad, superior or inferior.

Racism is an attitude that says, "Red [or white or brown or

black or yellow or chartreuse] is best because I say so." Scripture tells us simply to love our neighbors, regardless of their color, because in Christ all of us are equal. Besides, if we let it, such a various mix of people makes life more interesting—and the kingdom of God more effective.

The Word   Galatians 3:26-28

Discussion starters
1. Who are the outcast groups in your school?
2. How can you reach out to them so they know they are valuable to God?

3. Why do people decide that one race/flavor is superior to others?
4. What about people (who are made in the image of God) who have made decisions that violate God's image in us? How do we show acceptance of *who* they are without showing approval of *what* they do?

Life changers
1. Granted, it's a little too easy to talk in generalities about reaching out to people unlike us. So can you identify just one or two individuals with whom you can actually begin building a relationship?
2. Anyone you need to apologize to for something you said because they are different from you?

Holding On & Holding Out

The topic Priorities

The object About 20 quarters, and a jumbo-sized plastic Easter egg with a $20 bill inside with the word *God* written on the egg in dark ink. Write the letters large enough to stretch most of the way around the egg, so that the word isn't immediately readable unless you draw attention to it.

The lesson Spread out all the quarters on the table. Then tell a student volunteer that she can use only one hand (either her left or right, not both) to pick up as many quarters as she can hold in that hand. She must hold all the quarters in the hand she begins

with and may not lay down any quarters for any reason. The prize? She keeps all the money she's holding on to until the allotted time ends. (You may want to use this very phrasing with the volunteer, for subtle reasons you'll see in a moment.) Get the student to agree to the challenge, then pull the Easter egg out of your pocket and tell her the catch: she's got to pick up the quarters *while holding the plastic egg in the same hand.* If she wonders why a plastic egg, just tell her it's a test of dexterity and priorities—and don't explain it any further than that.

Then let the volunteer go for it...and as soon as she lets the plastic egg drop in her desire for more quarters, call time. Let the student return to her seat with her quarters. Then point out what's written on the plastic egg—*God*—open it, and display the $20 bill.

The game, of course, demonstrates how easy it is to loosen your grip on your relationship with God when you start clinging to other things that crowd him out. It's not that you want to toss away your commitment to Christ—it's just that you can get so involved in other stuff, other schedules, other people, other activities, that God gets crowded out. And your Christian commitment plummets. It comes down to either holding on to Jesus or holding out on him.

The Word   Matthew 6:19-34; Luke 12:33-34
See also Luke 14:15-24; Revelation 3:15-19; Haggai 1:9; Luke 18:18-25

Discussion starters

1. What did Jesus mean when he said, **"Where your treasure is, there your heart will be also" (Luke 12:34)?**

2. Why is it hard for a rich person to enter the kingdom of God (see Luke 18:25)?

Life changers

1. What do you tend to cling to that crowds God out?

2. Where is your treasure? *What* is your treasure?

3. If Jesus told you, "One thing you lack" (like he told the rich young ruler in Luke 18), what one thing would he be talking about?

One Key

The topic The uniqueness of Jesus

The object Lots of different kinds and sizes and shapes of keys—old-fashioned keys, keys on quirky key rings, a two-foot-long honorary key (as "a key to the city"), hotel keys (both the traditional kind and the plastic card kind with the electronic code); etc. Also have a lock which can be opened by one of the keys.

The lesson Each of these keys suggests an appealing quality. This key lets you into an ornate hotel room...this old key is itself ornate...this one hangs on a key ring you could *never* lose...this one promises shelter...this one is a ticket to a prestigious vehicle. But only this key...here... will open this lock.

There are many different ways to God, some say— **many ways to experience God. This certainly has some truth to it—but only as long as those**

ways go through Jesus. Which is what Jesus meant when he said, "I am the way."

He made claims about himself that no other leader has

made (imbeciles and egomaniacs, maybe, but not serious leaders). Jesus didn't say he pointed to the way, or that he knew the way, or even that he could teach the way. He said he *is* the way.

The Word   John 14:6; Acts 4:12
See also 1 Timothy 2:5-6

Discussion starters
1. Your English teacher explains, "Christianity is only one of many religions and philosophies that people have embraced over the years. Like most other belief systems, Christianity has both its benefits and its weaknesses." How would you respond?

2. History is full of individuals who said they were messiahs. Is there **any way to distinguish the claims of Jesus about himself from the claims of imbeciles and egomaniacs about themselves?**

3. How would you respond to someone who says, "Anyone who thinks Jesus is the *only* way is simply close-minded, narrow, and intolerant of any belief other than theirs"?

Life changers
1. Have you responded to this Jesus as if he were—
   ○ A liar
   ○ A lunatic
   ○ The Lord

Play-Doh, Play Dumb, Play Along

The topic Conformity

The object Play-Doh and a variety of molds.

The lesson Spend a few minutes describing the nature and uses of Play-Doh—while you're combining colors, making clay

snakes and bowls, and pressing the stuff into molds. (Let what you make be

determined by whatever is currently hot with your group–good -natured high school rivalries, finals week, a new youth pastor, the Summer or Winter Olympics, a presidential election, upcoming retreat or missions trip, etc.) Demonstrate that changing the shape does not necessarily alter its color and texture. And if you don't like what you make, you can always squish it to a pancake or roll it into a ball or cram it into a mold—and make something different.

We live in a culture that constantly tries to cram us into a mold, so we can be acceptable to those around us (when our culture says "acceptable," it means "just like everybody else"). Yet God tells us *not* to be shaped by the world, but instead to let the Word of God transform us into his image, from the inside out.

The Word Romans 12:1-2 (check out this passage in the J.B. Phillips version); Jeremiah 18:1-6
See also Isaiah 45:9; Isaiah 64

Discussion starters
1. What are some typical molds that students at your school get squeezed into?
2. Why do we give in so easily **to the Play-Doh culture that squeezes us into conformity?**
3. Why is it so difficult to put ourselves in God's hands and let *him* mold us instead?

Life changers
1. What kind of mold are you being squeezed into?
2. How would you describe the work of the Divine Potter in your life?
   ○ I'm just not letting God get his hands on my life right now.
   ○ I've said, "Okay, God, do your thing"—but he's working with some really hard material. I just don't mold easily.
   ○ God is trimming some rough edges off me so I'll fit his design for me better.
   ○ God's using circumstances to roll air bubbles out of my life.
   ○ Right now I'm feeling the heat in the kiln, but it's God in control, working circumstances to set me firmly in his design.

Coloring Outside the Lines

The topic A willingness to be different

The object A coloring book, or children's Sunday school take-home sheets that kids color. Most of the pictures need to have been colored by young children. Get your own preschooler to color up a bunch of pictures for you, or bribe the fours and fives Sunday school teacher for samples.

The lesson Pass around the coloring books or post the colored sheets. Spark some discussion about the characteristics of coloring-book art by very young artists: ghastly colors...bristly angles rather than easy curves...and, of course, little restraint at keeping one's crayon strokes within the lines.

While lines can give children some patterns and guidelines to work with, they're more likely to stifle creativity. Kids get so focused on

coloring **within the lines that they're afraid to produce any image other than the expected one.**

We tend to live the same way. Our culture pressures us to

stay in the lines, to use this or that color, to not even think of adding something new to the page that isn't already outlined. And too often we play along, wanting so desperately to fit in and not stand out. We're afraid of drawing attention to ourselves. Consequently, we have entire high schools of adolescents who are all coloring their lives with the same color of crayon. Dress this way; talk that way; act like this—stay in the lines, don't draw outside the lines. Even alternative kids, who are supposedly drawing outside the lines, end up all looking exactly alike.

God calls us to color outside the lines of a culture that conforms—and discover the freedom of letting him make our lives better than even a Monet.

The Word Romans 12:1-2; Numbers 14 (especially verse 24)
See also Matthew 5:3-5

Discussion starters

1. According to Numbers 14, how did Caleb and Joshua color outside the lines?
2. When we color outside the lines, our pictures don't look as neat and clean as everyone else's. But when a child brings home an outside the lines picture, how do the parents respond? What are the parents really celebrating when they put that picture on the refrigerator?
3. What are some of the lines at school you're expected to stay inside?
4. What's the difference between nonconformity and simply acting weird? Are there any lines we *should* stay inside of (for example, Romans 12:1-2; Exodus 20)?

Life changers

1. What for you is the scariest part of coloring outside the lines?
2. What do you think God would say about the picture you're drawing with your life?
3. Is God calling you to be a Joshua or a Caleb?

Letting God Give Us a Hand

The topic Christ in us

The object A glove, a ceramic cup or plate (If you do the Bonus activity, you'll need a glove for each student, with GALATIANS 2:20 written on each one. Check out a thrift store or Home Depot's bargain bin.)

The lesson By itself, this glove is dead and lifeless. On the outside, it looks nice; it might even be an expensive and **glamorous accessory. But an empty glove can't hold someone's hand (demonstrate this...easy to make humorous), it's**

absolutely useless for holding objects (try to put the cup or plate in the glove's hand, only to have it drop it—
the shattering is sure to get your kids' attention), and it has no way of arresting or even detecting a destructive act done to it (slap it against the wall, then use a lighter to set one of its fingers on fire...let it burn only a few moments before putting it out). In short, an empty glove is lifeless and, therefore, useless.

Which is precisely how the Scripture describes our lives

without Jesus Christ. We're dead in our sins without Jesus, unable to tell right and wrong, unable to love as God intends. By putting your hand in the glove—that is, by inviting Jesus to live his life inside of us—Christ gives us life. He is our hope and help.

The Word   Galatians 2:20; John 15:5-6
See also Colossians 1:27

Discussion starters
1. Using the glove analogy, what are some ways society tries to make an empty glove seem alive (educate the glove, affirm the glove for its glove qualities, pretend that being on fire is really okay, get mad at the glove, buy a new glove in hopes that *this* one will certainly be alive, etc.)?

2. What did the apostle Paul mean when he wrote, **"I have been crucified with Christ and I no longer live, but Christ lives in me"** (Galatians 2:20)?

3. How many hands can fit into a glove at one time? What does that tell you about the importance of giving control of your life to Jesus?

Life changers
1. Do you need to ask Jesus to live inside you? If you haven't, what's keeping you from it?

Bonus!
As a reminder of this lesson, give each student a glove with GALATIANS 2:20 written it.

Thou Shalt Knot

The topic The consequences of continued sin

The object. Three lengths of thread—two of them 3 yards long, and one just long enough to go around a pair of clasped hands and be tied off—and a pair of scissors.

The lesson Using the short piece of string, tie the hands of a student volunteer. Tie it snugly so it will stay on, but not so tight that it cuts into her hands. Once tied, ask the student to break free. (Unless you inadvertently used extra-heavy quilting thread, anyone should be able to break out easily.)

That was really impressive, tell her. Can she do it again? But this time wrap the entire three-yard length of thread

around her hands (that's 20 to 30 times). This time it will be virtually impossible. Ask for another student to come help her break out (using just his hands, no knife or scissors). He probably won't be able to help much. (20 to 30 rounds of thread is a virtual rope.)

Explain that this is how sin works in our lives. Little by little it enslaves us until we're trapped, tied to lifestyle patterns, consequences, and attitudes. Some of us look to our friends to help us break free—maybe they can help, maybe they can't. But Scripture tells us one sure way (though it's usually gradual) to break free from the bondage of sin: the power of Jesus. At this point use the scissors to cut loose your volunteer. If we confess our sins and ask him for help, Jesus will forgive us and give us the power to overcome sin.

The Word   1 John 1:9; Galatians 5:1,13-15
See also John 8:32-36; Isaiah 42:6-7

Discussion starters
1. What part of your life is tied up? What is the string that's tying it up?
2. Where do these strings come from? Are they tied on by us or by others?

Life changers
1. What are the strings in your life that don't seem too serious, but that could tie you up if you don't let Christ deal with them?
2. Based on the ideas we've discussed, which area of your life is most affected by your bondage?
3. How willing are you **to really let Jesus break the bondage and set you free?**

Connect the Dots

The topic Faith

The object A connect-the-dots puzzle

The lesson Doing a connect-the-dots puzzle is a little like practicing faith. (As you're explaining the lesson, be working the puzzle.) You begin by believing that an image really will be revealed—even though you have no idea what it is. In other words, you can't see the picture, but you

believe it's there. You trust that an artist designed a picture that will be revealed if you continue to trace the sequence, dot to dot. If you don't connect the dots in sequence, or if you decide to stop drawing, you'll never see the full picture the artist has designed.

So it is with your faith in God. You don't always see exactly where God is leading you... sometimes you have only part of the picture. But faith is when, in the words of one experienced Christian, we continue to trust God's heart even when we cannot trace his hand.

The Word   Hebrews 11:1-6

Discussion starters
1. Why can you trust that God has adequately planned the picture he is leading you to draw (for example, Hebrews 11:3)?
2. What happens to the picture when you begin disregarding the proper sequence of numbers?

Life changers
1. What kinds of problems have caused you to doubt God's design for the picture of your life? Seemingly missing numbers? Vague dots? Big gaps?
2. Can you see the dots well enough, but lately lost interest in joining them because you can't make sense of the image you're outlining?
3. Has there been a time recently when you've had to trust

God's heart even though you could not trace his hand? Take a moment now and thank God for his sovereignty and the grand design of your life.

Your Nose Knows

The topic The aroma of Christ

The object A collection of objects with intense or distinctive smells—deodorant, aftershave or perfume, scented candles, blue cheese, spoiled food, toothpaste, freshly mowed grass, dirty socks, kerosene, burnt toast, coffee beans, etc.

The lesson Conduct a contest among several kids to see who can identify the most smells—or give everyone a sniff and an opportunity to guess.

Odors can be either subtle or poignant, sensuous or repulsive. Our sense of smell brings us information and leaves us with specific impressions about a food, a room, a sweater, a body.

The apostle Paul reminds us that Christians have a

fragrance that tells passersby that we have a relationship with Christ, and that—like a hungry person who smells the aroma of soup and steak and pie coming from the kitchen—unbelievers will be drawn to Christ through us.

The Word   2 Corinthians 2:14-15

Discussion starters
1. What should a Christian smell like—spiritually speaking, that is?

2. Do you think most people consider the **aroma of Christians to be attractive or repugnant? Why?**

3. Why do you think that, when some Christians leave the room, everyone's holding their noses (for example, 2 Corinthians 2:17)?

Life changers
1. Most individuals use deodorant and scents—colognes or perfumes—to either enhance or camouflage their natural body scents. At what times do you worry about those around you smelling the natural fragrance of Christ in you—and so you camouflage the smell?

2. Which of the following statements describes your own personal fragrance:
- ○ Frankly, I don't think anyone can smell anything
- ○ Like roadkill
- ○ A little sour
- ○ Minty fresh
- ○ Too strong at times

Material World

The topic Wise money management

The object Monopoly money, and items to auction—stuff teenagers typically value, like certificates for fast food and free tutoring and computer instruction, candy, car washes, etc. If your group is up to a tongue-in-cheek twist, get parents to give you stuff they've salvaged off their kids' bedroom floors or closets or shelves—to win their items back, students must purchase them at the auction!

Distribute only enough money for each student to be able to purchase a few of the auctioned items. The point of this object lesson is the tension between many purchasing opportunities— and limited cash.

The lesson Distribute the money, then—as in real auctions— give kids at least five minutes to look over the stuff to be auctioned before bidding opens, so they can plan their strategies. When you open the bidding, students can either bid independently on an item or pool their cash for joint purchases.

You've heard it before, but it's still true: money doesn't grow on trees. Learning to make wise decisions about how you spend your money is a good discipline—even a spiritual principle—to learn and apply.

The Word   1Timothy 6:3-10, Proverbs 13:11
See also Matthew 19:16-30; Luke 12:13-21

Discussion starters

1. Did you get an allowance when you were younger? How much? How often? Did you have to earn the allowance? If so, how?

2. If you won $10 million, what would you do with the money? In what ways would that money change your life—and your relationships in particular?

3. Do you have a savings plan for what you earn or otherwise receive? What are you saving for?

4. What is dangerous about wanting to be rich?

Life changers

1. "Godliness with contentment is great gain," wrote St. Paul to the young church pastor Timothy (1 Timothy 6:6). On a scale of 1 to 10, how content are you (1 = very content, 10 = very discontent)? To what do you attribute your contentedness or discontent?

2. What is your biggest concern when you think about money and finances? Why?

3. If all jobs made the same **amount of income, what job would you like as an adult?**

4. Do you sometimes feel that God may be prompting you to make a change about money and material possessions? If so, can you put your finger on just what that change could be?

5. What do you think St. Paul meant when he wrote to Timothy that "people who want to get rich fall into temptation and a trap"? Do you feel like money traps *you*? How?

What's Weighing You Down?

The topic Spiritual endurance

The object Heavy weights like bricks or large rocks.

The lesson Get out the Ideas Library's *Games 2 for Youth Groups*, find the "Relay Races" section, and select a few that fit your setting. For this object lesson, you want relay races that are simple and familiar, rather than complicated or exotic. Explain the rules, get the kids ready to play—then just before the starting whistle, say something like, "Oh, yeah—almost forgot to tell you that you've all got to do this relay race carrying this (oomph) bag o' bricks (whew)," or large stones, or other heavy (though safe) weight. (Instead of extra weight, you can burden them by requiring jumping jacks, running in place, sit ups, or knee bends at various times in the race. But carrying weights makes your point clearer.)

Your students will not only see, but *experience* that simple tasks are more difficult when they carry extra weight.

The Word   Hebrew 12:1-3, Philippians 3:12-14

Discussion starters

1. What kind of unnecessary weight are you carrying in your race of faith? What would you have to do to shed it?

2. Are there any reasons why a person would have *wanted* to be slowed down in this relay race—or in the race of faith?

Life changers

1. New fabrics and materials—from shoe construction to bike components—are invented precisely to lighten a racer's weight. Athletes depend on these high-tech innovations to shave race-winning tenths and hundredths of a second off their time. Think of your life now . . . imagine that you threw off some weights that were slowing you down in your spiritual race. What kind of "lighter" habits or disciplines could you then put *on* that would increase your spiritual stamina and endurance, that would let you run farther and faster without getting exhausted?

2. What kind of help can you expect if you become serious about shedding this kind of weight?

3. Picture your relationship with Christ as a race. Where are you—in **the locker room, in set position waiting for the starting gun to go off, approaching the finish line, a spectator in the stands, or—?**

Who Named You Judge?

The topic Do not judge others

The object Watermelons, knife, several pairs of tweezers

The lesson Cut up small sections of watermelon. Tell your students they can have a piece of watermelon—if, after they take a *big* bite of seedy watermelon, they can 1) separate the seeds from the fruit *in their mouth*, using nothing but teeth, tongue, and palate; and 2) keep *all* the seeds in their mouth until they swallow the fruit, then spit them out all at one time.

Here's a less messy option that can also involve more students. (It's a little less to the point, but a lot of fun.) Divide students into equal-sized teams of 10 or less. Have them sit in a large circle with a half or a quarter watermelon in the middle of them. On "Go!" the first person on each team sprints to the watermelon in the middle of her circle and plucks out as many watermelon seeds as she can in the allotted time, using only the tweezers. Add seconds or deduct points for removing too much fruit as players dig out seeds.

Every 10 seconds or so, yell, "Switch!" at which time the next person in the circle takes over. Continue the game until everyone on the team has had a turn or two.

Seeds make watermelon eating inconvenient. All watermelon seeds seem to do is get in the way of enjoying the fruit. They distract you from the flavor.

So what gets in the way of others enjoying the sweetness of

your spirit, of your company? Have a few seeds in your personality? Maybe a critical spirit? In conversations you tend to belittle ideas that aren't yours? Or maybe you dominate conversations . . . after all, you *are* right about things most of the time, aren't you?

So get rid of some of these seeds, already! Let others enjoy the good fruit of your friendship without the distractions.

The Word   Matthew 7:1-5

Discussion starters
1. Name a person in your life that you feel accepts you for who you are—seeds and all.

2. Name a person that you feel **judges you and tries to change who you are. (You feel they're trying too hard or in the wrong ways to get rid of your seeds?)**

3. Jesus talked about not trying to remove a tiny speck from your friend's eye when you have a huge plank in your own. Why did Jesus feel this advice was important to the people who followed him?

Life changers
1. Name a few seeds in your life.
2. If Jesus were to hang out with you and your group of friends, what do you think he would say or do to help your group better reflect his love?

Labels & Lies

The topic Deceptive appearances

The object A can opener, a small can of tuna, and the label off a similarly sized can of cat food. (*Don't* get the white kind of tuna—in fact, the more it looks like cat food, the better.) Before the meeting, replace the tuna label with the cat-food label.

The lesson Tell your students dramatically how much you love to eat. (If they know you as a finicky eater, reveal this "fact" as one of your best-kept secrets.) As you explain the lengths you go to to satisfy your appetite, open the can with the cat food label. While you eat the meat and sip the juice from the can, go into great detail about the nutrients, great flavor, and cost-effectiveness of

eating cat food. ("Really, it's not that bad . . .tastes kinda like chicken. Anyone want to try a bite?")

Don't be fooled by appearances. Things aren't always what they appear.

The Word   Acts 10:1-23

Discussion starters

1. Name a vegetable you simply hate.

2. Name the different groups of students that **eat together in the lunch room at your school. What do their appearances tell you about them? What <u>don't</u> their appearances tell you about them?**

3. If Jesus were to be a student for a day at your school, which group would he eat lunch with?

Life changers

1. Imagine you chaired a student body committee that was in charge of prescribing punishment for kids who were caught fighting. Who would you choose to be on that committee with you? Why? How would you determine the punishment?

2. How important is the appearance factor in choosing a friend, regardless of whether you or your friend is male or female?

3. How can you help the walls come down between certain cliques at your school or even in your youth group?

Mastering the Map

The topic Guidance

The object Identical maps, one for each group of 2 to 5 people.

The lesson If your youth group is large, divide into smaller groups of 6 to 12. Distribute maps of your own city to each group, then explain the challenge: each group must find and mark where on the maps your church is, where each group member's home is, and the shortest (not necessarily quickest) route from church to each group member's home, and back to church. Afterward, informally poll each group to determine which group has the longest round trip, the shortest, etc.

Maps help us find our way. They give **direction and perspective. It can be easy in life to cruise along, doing your own thing, heading in no certain or deliberate direction** at all. Enter the Bible—it's as necessary a map for life as the one AAA gives you for your vacation.

The Word 2 Timothy 3:16; Psalm 119:133

Discussion starters
1. Ever ride with a driver who got lost because he couldn't or didn't use a map?

2. How many years can you use a map—highway map, topographical map, tourist map—before its accuracy suffers?

Life changers
1. What kind of a map is the Bible?

2. How trustworthy a map do you feel the Bible is? Why?

3. What about the Bible—or about your life—makes you wonder sometimes if the Bible-map is a little outdated?

Some prep, for big results

You may have to make a phone call or two to get your hands on these objects. Then again, they just might be sitting in your closet or garage.

Senior Year

The topic Our value

The object A high school yearbook—specifically, the senior pictures and the individual list of seniors' activities during their high school years, like this:

> French club, 10, 11, 12; soccer, 11, 12; student government, 10

If seniors' pictures and their lists of activities are in separate sections, cut and paste a sample page together. For extra effect try enlarging one or two of the senior pictures into overhead transparencies or PowerPoint slides.

The lesson When you flip through this yearbook and see pictures of graduating seniors and their activities, you can quickly

see that some were involved in almost everything— and others in almost nothing. And it's human nature to assume that the winners were the ones with the long list, and the losers were the ones with one-item lists like "Perfect attendance, 11."

But what is it that *really* makes our lives valuable? The Bible reminds us that no honor or activity is worth anything compared to the privilege of having a relationship with Christ and serving him.

The Word   Philippians 3:3-9

Discussion starters
1. What kind of activities give (or would give) you prestige and recognition on your campus?
2. If it were possible to design the perfect senior profile, what would it be?
3. Think of the list St. Paul wrote for himself in Philippians 3:5-6 as his senior yearbook activity list: "Circumcised on the eighth day, of the people of Israel, of the tribe of Benjamin, a Hebrew of Hebrews; in regard to the law, a Pharisee; as for zeal, persecuting the church; as for legalistic righteousness, faultless"—but none of it ranked in importance, he concluded, with "the surpassing worth of knowing Christ and being found in him." What about you? How do you know if you're putting too much emphasis on what makes it into yearbooks and scores with college scouts and college admissions counselors, and too little on the kind of stuff that counts in the kingdom of God? Or is it even as a matter of emphasis, or is it all or nothing?

Life changers
1. Are there any goals or activities in your life that you're counting on to build what Paul calls "confidence in the flesh"?

2. Imagine that upon graduation from this life to the next, **you get your photo and list of activities in your Life Yearbook. What would people say were your priorities based on your "activities list"? What would you want listed under your photo?**
3. What are you doing *now* to reflect your priorities? Do you need to shift your activities to reflect your priorities better?

Keep Your Head above Water

The topic Security

The object A Coast Guard-approved life jacket (you know, like the big orange U-shaped ones). If you want to be overt about the lesson, label this jacket JESUS CHRIST. You also need a variety of other (and unapproved) floatation devices, like inflatable rings, sea horses, floaties, rafts, etc. All the flotation devices should be inflated. In an inconspicuous place, label each of the "unapproved" ones with a different way people try to stay afloat in life—friendship, money, popularity, status, alcohol, athletic achievement, etc.

The lesson Let students model all the jackets, preservers, floaties, etc., then vote on which one they like best. Next, reveal **that these flashy, colorful, fun floats symbolize friendship, money, etc.— and that we too** often try to keep ourselves afloat with these. *Then* point out the simple, easily missed warning that comes with most flotation devices: *not* to use them as life-saving devices. Finally, demonstrate that the Coast Guard-approved life jacket isn't fun or stylish, and doesn't come in a choice of designer colors—yet it's the only one that you can count on to keep a person from drowning.

Scripture points us to the only Lifesaver who, in any crisis or storm, will keep our heads above water. A relationship with Jesus might not be as stylish or as fun-looking as a relationship with a bottle or a boyfriend or girlfriend. But in the end only Jesus will be enough to keep us from going under.

The Word   Psalm 20:1-9; Matthew 14:29-32
See also Job 31:24-28; Isaiah 31:1; Psalm 31:4-8; 40:3; 49:6

Discussion starters
1. What kind of "floatation devices" do people wear around your school?
2. Why is it so difficult to hear the Bible's warning that, when storms come, "toy" life preservers can't be counted on to keep our heads above water?
3. Why are we so reluctant to cling to the guaranteed Life Preserver? What kinds of things make it less attractive than inferior floatation devices?
4. If Jesus is the only real life preserver, what is it that he preserves us from? Does he promise Christians that they'll never have to go down with the ship?

Life changers
1. What floatation devices are you clinging to?
2. Complete this sentence: *Sometimes life can be rough, and it's hard to keep my head above water, but at least I know I've got—*
3. Which of the following statements describes you right now:

○ **I feel like I'm going under.**
○ I'm keeping my head above water for now, but only by clinging to untrustworthy stuff.
○ My friends are clinging to me, and I'm afraid they're going to drag us all under.
○ I'm clinging to the real Life Preserver.
○ I'm clinging to the real Life Preserver, but I keep wondering if there's a slow leak somewhere, or that I'll lose my grip in a storm.

Beautiful Feet

The topic A firm stand and consistent walk, two characteristics of committed disciples

The object Take pictures of the bare feet of students in your youth group. For fun, also throw in a few gag pictures, such as animal feet, baby feet, big clown's shoes, two feet side-by-side but facing in opposite directions. Make the pictures into enlargements, slides, overhead transparencies, or computer-generated images so the pictures are large enough for the group to view at the same time. These will be your beautiful feet pageant.

The lesson Show the pictures and let your students guess whose feet are whose or vote for the most beautiful feet.
       The Scripture speaks over and over about feet. In fact, it

talks almost as much about our feet as it does our hearts and our eyes. That's because the feet tell us two very important facts about someone: where she's standing and which

way she's going. A firm stand and a consistent walk in the direction of obedience are two key characteristics of a committed disciple of Jesus.

The Word Isaiah 52:7; Psalm 40:1-2; 56:13
See also Psalm 119:101-105; Hebrews 12:12-13

Discussion starters

1. We read in these passages about two grave dangers for feet: slipping and stumbling. What are some of the slippery spots around your school? What are some of the reasons a teenage Christian might stumble?

2. What are some of the practical steps you as a believer can take to strengthen your stand and straighten your walk?

3. Taking a strong stand isn't always easy. If someone in your school were to try to have "beautiful feet," what are some reasons she might have to step on some toes?

Life changers

1. Write yourself a *foot-note*, a short letter to yourself about some slippery spots and uneven places that you need to watch out for.

Lean on Thee

The topic Trusting God in the middle of pain and struggle

The object A variety of canes and crutches, maybe even a walker. If your church's elderly don't want to part with them, you can always buy 'em at a thrift store. Try to get a baby walker, too—the suspended seat on wheels babies propel themselves around in before they can walk.

The lesson As you show all the canes and crutches and walkers you've brought, give a short explanation about how they're used . . . the variety of ailments, disabilities, injuries, etc., that cause people to need them . . . the common function *all* the devices have: those who need the help can lean on them.

The Bible says that God is the one you can lean on when you're hurt or broken or tired or just can't keep your balance. He can support you and keep you from falling—*if* you lean on him.

The Word   Psalm 37:23-24; 1 Peter 5:6-7
See also Isaiah 35:3-6; Jude 24-25 (This passage might be a good closing prayer or benediction)

Discussion starters
1. What are the basic requirements of a good cane or crutch (see Proverbs 25:19)?
2. Some people say Christianity is totally lame, and all the talk about God is nothing but a crutch. What do you say to that?
3. What are some ways that even strong, fit, and in shape people are crippled on the inside?
4. Say we agree that Christianity is a crutch. What other crutches do people use to make their way through life? Does *everyone* have a crutch of some sort?

Life changers
1. What are you leaning on to help you make it through?
2. What disability of the soul might you have that weighs you down or makes it hard for you to walk in freedom and strength?
3. If you're a little reluctant to lean on Christ and put the full weight of your burdens on him, why?

Ripple Effect

The topic Consequences of sin

The object To illustrate ripples, you'll need a grapefruit (write SIN on it) and a lake or swimming pool or baptismal font or washtub—*anything* that will hold water, however little of it you can get. Of course, the more water, the better—a lake is better than a pail.

The lesson Lob the grapefruit out into the lake as far as you can—or, if you're using a more modest quantity of water, drop the grapefruit into the *middle* of the bucket. The point your kids should see is that, although the grapefruit actually touched only a very, very small spot in the lake, the ripples roll out for possibly hundreds of feet. And that's only what we can see—theoretically, the ripples touch the surface of the entire lake.

It's the same with sin. **We'd like to believe that our actions really don't affect anyone else all that much, and that therefore we should be able to do**

pretty much what we please. But Scripture and real life teach us otherwise: our actions *do* affect others. A mother's alcoholism affects her entire family. A teenage driver paying more attention to the conversation in the car than to the road causes the death of her passengers. A couple who has sex risks not only affecting a life, but *creating* one.

You can choose whether to sin or not. Unfortunately, you *can't* choose whether there will be ripples and consequences of your sin. There *will* be ripples, and somehow they will inevitably affect others.

The Word
Galatians 5:7-9; Exodus 20:5-6
See also Romans 5:12-21; Lamentations 5:7

Discussion starters
1. You know the almost automatic response that pops up in your head when you hear a parent, friend, or youth pastor say, "You can't do that." You typically respond, "It's *my* life." In light of the ripple effect, how true is that statement?
2. You may have heard it said, "The fruit doesn't fall far from the tree." How does that saying compare with lesson of the ripple effect?

Life changers
1. Name some people affected by the ripples of your decisions.

2. The ripple effect is true for both **positive and negative choices you make. What can you do this week to make some positive ripples from your life?**

Serious prep for special events

If you have these objects around the house, you're either a crackpot or a felon. To borrow them, you'll need to put on your suave salesperson persona. Or have a connection. But the  dynamite effect on your kids is worth the considerable preparation. You'll probably want to save these for big or special events.

Dam That Cursing!

The topic The way we talk

The object First, find someone who owns, manages, or works in a garden shop or nursery. Use your connections to borrow a fountain (be prepared to leave a deposit), or you just may want to buy a small, table-top model ($15 and up). Or simply hold this meeting at a home with a fountain. Any fountain will do—but a water-spewing cherub best suits the purposes of this object lesson. Have the fountain in full view, plugged in, and flowing while you're giving the object lesson. Start the lesson with white milk running through the fountain, then at the appropriate time be ready to add chocolate milk or a similarly colored liquid— anything, really, that makes the white-as-snow milk look dirty and scummy.

A warning is in order here. Before doing the object lesson, test the milk and chocolate milk on the bottom of the fountain to make sure they don't stain. Otherwise be prepared to go back to the gardening store and buy their lovely white and brown fountain.

The lesson Point out your lovely fountain (running white milk) and ask for a volunteer to drink from it. (Be prepared to be your own volunteer.) Then inconspicuously add the chocolate milk—and ask if someone would be willing to take a drink *now*.

The Scripture teaches that God takes our speech seriously.

To have obscene and flippantly foul language come out of the mouth of a Christian is as confusing to people as when a fountain pumps out nasty-looking fluids. No one takes a chance drinking from a dirty fountain, and no one is refreshed by grimy speech.

The Word   James 3:7-12; Matthew 12:33-37

Discussion starters
1. Why do you think God takes the words of our speech seriously?
2. What kinds of foul speech can spoil our fountain?
3. What are some practical steps a person can take to dam up a free-flowing habit of foul speech?

Life changers
1. What assumptions might your friends make about the source of your speech based on the words that come out of your mouth?
2. What conditions make your speech fountain turn foul?

Grave Considerations

The topic Making our lives count

The object Some kind of grave marker. Check the yellow pages (you'll be more likely to find listings under *memorials* than *tombstones*). Find a business that displays grave markers or memorial markers, and arrange to borrow one—or make a simple wooden or clay marker (or get a handyman from the Sunday school class of retirees to make one). If you're making your own, enscribe on it one of the epitaphs on this page.

FYI, you can find *lots* more epitaphs in places like these:
- *Epitaphs*, Nigel Rees (Carroll & Graf, 1994)
- *The Sunny Side of Genealogy*, compiled by Fonda D. Baselt
- On the Web at www.ancestory.com

The lesson With the grave marker center stage, read some of the gag epitaphs. Then for the segue: sooner or later, remind your students, all of you will die (unless you're a pretribulational dispensationalist, in

B. ARNOLD
COLD IS MY BED, BUT
OH, I LOVE IT,
FOR COLDER ARE MY
FRIENDS ABOVE IT.

PEGLEG PETE, THE
RIVER PIRATE,
WALKED THE PLANK
AND SANK.

REST IN PEACE
MOONSHINE LENNY
SEEMS HE TOOK ONE
DRINK TOO MANY.

BOBBY LEE SAID HIS CAR
WOULDN'T SKID
THIS TOMBSTONE SHOWS
THAT IT COULD AND DID.

A NEAR-SIGHTED
MINER IN SHAFT 39
LIT HIS CIGAR AND
BLEW UP THE MINE.

RED HOT HARRY
HE GOT HOT
BUT HE WAS SLOW
SO HE GOT PUT SIX
FEET BELOW.

FLORA FINCH
SWEPT AWAY
BY APRIL SHOWERS,
HERE SHE LIES
BENEATH THE FLOWERS.

IT WAS BECAUSE OF A COUGH
THAT THEY CARRIED HIM OFF
IT WAS A COFFIN THEY
CARRIED HIM OFF IN.

which case some will *not* die, but be "raptured" instead). And when you do, **someone will probably put a concrete marker over your grave (or a plaque on your mausoleum crypt, or the urn of ashes on the mantle).**

So what kind of epitaph might someone write on your gravestone or plaque—one simple phrase—that sums up all your years? HAD A VERY COOL CAR . . . LOOKED AWESOME IN A BATHING SUIT . . . MADE A TON OF MONEY . . . YOU WOULDN'T BELIEVE WHAT HE COULD DO ON A SKATEBOARD. OR THIS LIFE TOUCHED MANY FOR GOOD . . . SHE BROUGHT JOY TO ALL SHE MET . . . HE NEVER WAS RICH, BUT HE HAD A FAMILY THAT LOVED HIM, FRIENDS THAT RESPECTED HIM, AND THE PROMISE OF ETERNAL LIFE . . . WELL DONE GOOD AND FAITHFUL SERVANT

The Word Matthew 16:26; 1 John 2:15-17

Discussion starters
1. What makes a life to have been worthwhile when it's over?
2. What does it mean to "not love the world or anything in the world"?
3. What did Jesus mean about a person who "forfeits his soul"?

Life changers
1. An old hymn goes like this: "Only one life, 'twil soon be passed / Only what's done for Christ will last." What did you do last week that will actually last?
2. Write a phrase you'd like people to read—one that would sum up your life at the end of it.

Cramming for the Final

The topic Material possessions and eternal significance

The object A coffin. So check out your connections in funeral homes and coffin dealers. (Just don't tell them you're dying to borrow one . . . they've heard that line too many times.) Without such a connection, it's probably easier to bring your youth group to a funeral home (or coffin dealer) and conduct this meeting there. Inside the coffin put several toys; choose at least some of them for their symbolic value—a Barbie doll (obsession with style and with unattainable thinness), a Matchbox Jaguar or BMW or Porsche (prestigious wheels), a dumbbell or other workout weight (a buff body), a computer mouse (for today's electronic "toys") . . . you get the idea. Add some that particularly connect with your group.

The lesson You've seen the bumper sticker that says HE WHO DIES WITH THE MOST TOYS WINS. Ask your students to imagine **themselves, a couple or three decades from now, lying in a coffin (like this one).** Open the coffin, say something like "Well, look at the toys *this* person died with," and pull them out one at a time with a few words about what the toys symbolize. Close with something like "So *this* is what the world calls winning? Does this look like winning to you?"

What the Bible calls "winning" is laying up treasures for yourself in heaven—investing in something bigger than your own toys, and giving your life to something more lasting than earthly riches.

The Word   Matthew 6:19-21; Luke 12:16-26
See also Psalm 49:16-19

Discussion starters
1. What do you think of the HE WHO DIES WITH THE MOST TOYS WINS bumper sticker? How would it read if you were to change it?

2. What are some of the **toys we're supposed to be collecting if we want to be winners in the eyes of the world?**

3. What are some ways we can store up treasures in heaven?

4. Rewrite the parable of the rich fool in Luke 12:16-26. As you write, try to imagine how it would be if D. Rich Fool were a student in your school. If not barns and crops, what would he keep on building and amassing?

Life changers
1. Imagine that a secret observer watched everything you did and said last month. What kind of toys would the observer say you're collecting?

2. What is one specific way you can make an eternal investment this week?

Stop, Caution, Yield, Merge

The topic Making godly decisions

The object Two traffic signs: a stop, speed limit, or do-not-enter sign; and a merge, yield, or caution sign. You may be able to get the signs without committing a felony if you talk to your high school's driver education teacher or ask the Department of Motor Vehicles Safety Division.

You may also want to make a "stop sign" that says NO ADULTERY (Exodus 20:14), and a "yield sign" that says DON'T PUT OBSTACLES IN ANOTHER CHRISTIAN'S PATH (Romans 14:13).

The lesson God gives us two kinds of guidance in the Bible—precepts and principles.

Stop signs, speed limit signs, and do not enter signs are *precept* signs—they give us

very definite, specific commands about what we should or should not do. When  the sign says 65 miles per hour, it means exactly that. It doesn't mean 65 miles per hour unless I'm running late, or 65 unless the driver is listening to a cool song on the radio. You can always drive faster than 65, but this sign states that, if you disregard the precept, you risk paying for it.

In a similar way, the Ten Commandments are precepts. When the Bible forbids adultery, it doesn't mean no adultery unless you're *really* in love and she's beautiful and you've been dating her for five months. You break this precept, you may have a price to pay.

Principles, on the other hand, are like the merge, yield, and caution signs. They let you know that something tricky is ahead— but they *don't* tell you exactly what to do about it. Similarly, parts of the Bible say in so many words, "There's the goal, and here are the boundaries—now *you* make the call." A command like "Don't put obstacles in another Christian's path" doesn't tell you what exact obstacles you're to avoid putting in another's path (pornographic Web sites? unnecessary controversies? a messy bedroom? chocolate?)—but it *does* let you know that, whatever the specifics are (and they could be anything), don't get in the way of someone else, making life more difficult than it already is (as *The Message* puts it). Then *we* have to decide how to apply this principle.

The Word Psalm 119:4, 9-12, 15, 66

Discussion starters
1. What other examples of biblical precepts can you think of?
2. Read, distribute, or post the following verses. Ask your kids to a) work out the implied principles, and b) give practical examples of how the principles might be worked out in real life:
- Romans 14:13-18
- 1 Corinthians 6:19-20
- 1 Timothy 4:12
- Philippians 4:8
- 2 Corinthians 6:14-18

3. Why does God give us both precepts *and* principles? Why do you think we need both?

Life changers
1. Which type of sin do you need to start taking more seriously— a sin that violates a Bible *precept* or a Bible *principle*?
2. Of the principles you've looked at in this study, which do you consider most important on the spiritual road you're traveling?
3. How would your life be different this next week if you allowed your journey to be guided by this principle?

Resources from Youth Specialties

Professional Resources

Administration, Publicity, & Fundraising (Ideas Library)

Equipped to Serve: Volunteer Youth Worker Training Course

Help! I'm a Junior High Youth Worker!

Help! I'm a Small-Group Leader!

Help! I'm a Sunday School Teacher!

Help! I'm a Volunteer Youth Worker!

How to Expand Your Youth Ministry

How to Speak to Youth...and Keep Them Awake at the Same Time

Junior High Ministry (Updated & Expanded)

The Ministry of Nurture: A Youth Worker's Guide to Discipling Teenagers

Purpose-Driven Youth Ministry

Purpose-Driven Youth Ministry Training Kit

So That's Why I Keep Doing This! 52 Devotional Stories for Youth Workers

A Youth Ministry Crash Course

The Youth Worker's Handbook to Family Ministry

Youth Ministry Programming

Camps, Retreats, Missions, & Service Ideas (Ideas Library)

Compassionate Kids: Practical Ways to Involve Your Students in Mission and Service

Creative Bible Lessons from the Old Testament

Creative Bible Lessons in 1&2 Corinthians

Creative Bible Lessons in John: Encounters with Jesus

Creative Bible Lessons in Romans: Faith on Fire!

Creative Bible Lessons on the Life of Christ

Creative Bible Lessons in Psalms

Creative Junior High Programs from A to Z, Vol. 1 (A-M)

Creative Junior High Programs from A to Z, Vol. 2 (N-Z)

Creative Meetings, Bible Lessons, & Worship Ideas (Ideas Library)

Crowd Breakers & Mixers (Ideas Library)

Downloading the Bible Leader's Guide

Drama, Skits, & Sketches (Ideas Library)

Drama, Skits, & Sketches 2 (Ideas Library)

Dramatic Pauses

Everyday Object Lessons

Games (Ideas Library)

Games 2 (Ideas Library)

Good Sex: A Whole-Person Approach to Teenage Sexuality & God

Great Fundraising Ideas for Youth Groups

More Great Fundraising Ideas for Youth Groups

Great Retreats for Youth Groups

Holiday Ideas (Ideas Library)

Hot Illustrations for Youth Talks

More Hot Illustrations for Youth Talks

Still More Hot Illustrations for Youth Talks

Ideas Library on CD-ROM

Incredible Questionnaires for Youth Ministry

Junior High Game Nights

More Junior High Game Nights

Kickstarters: 101 Ingenious Intros to Just about Any Bible Lesson

Live the Life! Student Evangelism Training Kit

The Next Level Leader's Guide

Memory Makers

Play It! Over 150 Great Games for Youth Groups

Roaring Lambs

Special Events (Ideas Library)

Spontaneous Melodramas

Student Leadership Training Manual

Student Underground: An Event Curriculum on the Persecuted Church

Super Sketches for Youth Ministry

Talking the Walk

Teaching the Bible Creatively

What Would Jesus Do? Youth Leader's Kit

Wild Truth Bible Lessons

Wild Truth Bible Lessons 2

Wild Truth Bible Lessons: Pictures of God

Worship Services for Youth Groups

Discussion Starters

Discussion & Lesson Starters (Ideas Library)

Discussion & Lesson Starters 2 (Ideas Library)

Edge TV

Get 'Em Talking

Keep 'Em Talking!

High School TalkSheets

More High School TalkSheets

High School TalkSheets: Psalms and Proverbs

Junior High TalkSheets

More Junior High TalkSheets

Junior High TalkSheets: Psalms and Proverbs

Real Kids: Short Cuts

Real Kids: The Real Deal on Friendship, Loneliness, Racism, & Suicide

Real Kids: The Real Deal on Sexual Choices, Family Matters, & Loss

Real Kids: The Real Deal on Stressing Out, Addictive Behavior, Great Comebacks, & Violence

Real Kids: Word on the Street

Unfinished Sentences: 450 Tantalizing Statement-Starters to Get Teenagers Talking & Thinking

What If...? 450 Thought-Provoking Questions to Get Teenagers Talking, Laughing, and Thinking

Would You Rather...? 465 Provocative Questions to Get Teenagers Talking

Have You Ever...? 450 Intriguing Questions Guaranteed to Get Teenagers Talking

Art Source Clip Art

Stark Raving Clip Art (print)

Youth Group Activities (print)

Clip Art Library Version 2.0 (CD-ROM)

Digital Resources

Clip Art Library Version 2.0 (CD-ROM)

Ideas Library on CD-ROM

Videos

EdgeTV

Equipped to Serve: Volunteer Youth Worker Training Course

The Heart of Youth Ministry: A Morning with Mike Yaconelli

Good Sex: A Whole-Person Approach to Teenage Sexuality & God

Purpose-Driven Youth Ministry Training Kit

Real Kids: Short Cuts

Real Kids: The Real Deal on Friendship, Loneliness, Racism, & Suicide

Real Kids: The Real Deal on Sexual Choices, Family Matters, & Loss

Real Kids: The Real Deal on Stressing Out, Addictive Behavior, Great Comebacks, & Violence

Real Kids: Word on the Street

Student Underground: An Event Curriculum on the Persecuted Church

Understanding Your Teenager Video Curriculum

Student Books

Downloading the Bible: A Rough Guide to the New Testament

Downloading the Bible: A Rough Guide to the Old Testament

Grow For It Journal

Grow For It Journal through the Scriptures

What Almost Nobody Will Tell You About Sex

What Would Jesus Do? Spiritual Challenge Journal

Spiritual Challenge Journal: The Next Level

Teen Devotional Bible

Wild Truth Journal for Junior Highers

Wild Truth Journal: Pictures of God